My Hands

By Adriana Diaz-Donoso

Illustrated by Marjolein Francois

Library For All Ltd.

Library For All is an Australian not for profit organisation with a mission to make knowledge accessible to all via an innovative digital library solution. Visit us at libraryforall.org

My Hands

This edition published 2022

Published by Library For All Ltd
Email: info@libraryforall.org
URL: libraryforall.org

Library For All gratefully acknowledges the contributions of all who made previous editions of this book possible.

Original illustrations by Marjolein Francois

My Hands
Diaz-Donoso, Adriana
ISBN: 978-1-922827-47-0
SKU02664

My Hands

I have two hands.

When I play outside,
my hands can get dirty.

When I finish playing,
I wash them with soap.

I use soap because it cleans my hands very well. It kills worms and germs.

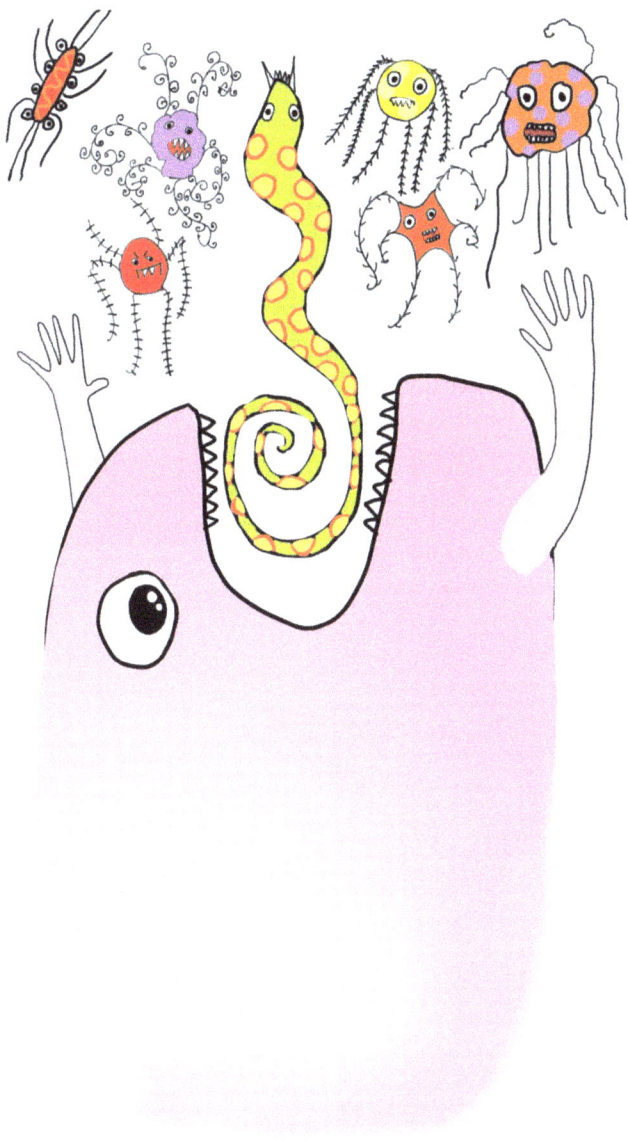

I also wash my hands
with soap before eating.

My hands need to be clean to keep me safe, so I can grow healthy.

I always wash my hands with soap. I hope you do the same, too.

You can use these questions to talk about this book with your family, friends and teachers.

What did you learn from this book?

Describe this book in one word. Funny? Scary? Colourful? Interesting?

How did this book make you feel when you finished reading it?

What was your favourite part of this book?

download our reader app
getlibraryforall.org

About the contributors

Library For All works with authors and illustrators from around the world to develop diverse, relevant, high quality stories for young readers. Visit libraryforall.org for the latest news on writers' workshop events, submission guidelines and other creative opportunities.

Did you enjoy this book?

We have hundreds more expertly curated original stories to choose from.

We work in partnership with authors, educators, cultural advisors, governments and NGOs to bring the joy of reading to children everywhere.

Did you know?

We create global impact in these fields by embracing the United Nations Sustainable Development Goals.

www.ingramcontent.com/pod-product-compliance
Lightning Source LLC
Chambersburg PA
CBHW040321050426
42452CB00018B/2955